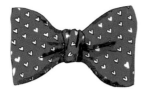

the BOW TIE book

Illustrations by James Gulliver Hancock

UNIVERSE

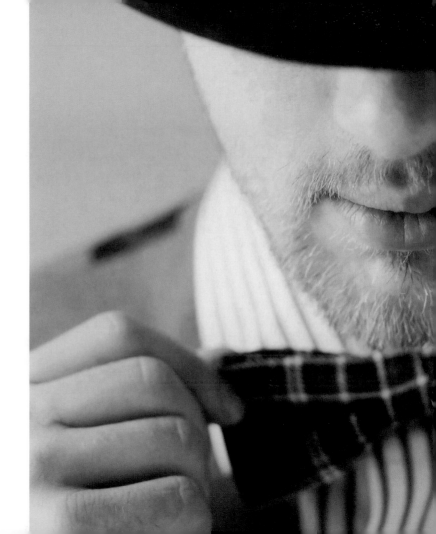

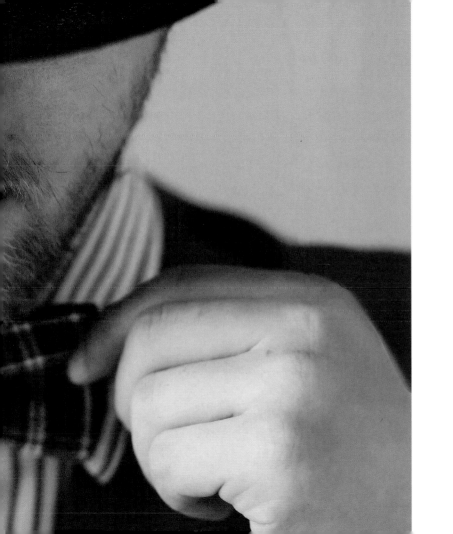

The History of the Bow Tie

*I*conoclastic yet conservative, fussily formal but offbeat, geeky but increasingly chic, the bow tie has been evolving at the upper echelons of society ever since the seventeenth century. Now freed from its strict ceremonial status, the accessory has become a fashion statement of discernment.

The bow tie had military, practical, and romantic origins: Its ancestor was a narrow scarf worn by Croatian cavalry mercenaries to bind their shirt collars together for identification in battle and to conserve body heat. In addition, often the scarves were gifted to the horsemen by their loved ones in Croatia, as keepsakes of safe return.

After King Louis XIII hired these mercenaries to fight the Habsburg Empire during the Thirty Years' War (1618–48), French soldiers picked up the style. The flowy "à la Croate" or "la cravate" replaced the rigid, ornate ruff collars worn at the time. Louis XIII named later Croatian mercenary regiments the Royal-Cravates.

In exile in France, King Charles II embraced the neckwear style and brought it to England when his monarchy was restored. Cravats became trendy in the upper classes of England and the American colonies.

Then, in the early 1800s, Emperor Napoleon Bonaparte decreed that his military officers must wear white satin breeches at ceremonial events. Napoleon's edict may have inspired Western civilization's most formal men's dress code, which was standardized in England by dandy George "Beau" Brummell. Brummell established evening dress as a tailored dark coat, full-length trousers, a white waistcoat, and an elaborate cravat. The cravat was soon simplified and formalized into a white bow tie, which gave the style its name, "white tie." Under King George IV, the outfit became official, and, throughout the monarchy of William IV and the prosperous, conservative reign of Queen Victoria, it was the required uniform of the Western world at evening ceremonial occasions.

According to some sources, in October of 1886, an American tobacco manufacturer named Nathaniel Griswold Lorillard first wore an adjusted white-tie outfit, with a cropped tailcoat and black bow tie, to a ball at his family's estate in Tuxedo Park, New York. Other sources claim that a coffee

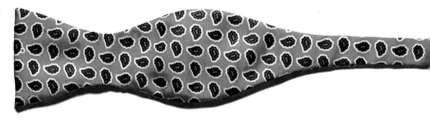

broker named James Potter brought the new style to Tuxedo Park. In any case, the outfit became known as "black tie" or a "tuxedo," a fashion that has now all but replaced white tie at upscale events.

Bow ties gained color by the 1950s, with midnight-blue, maroon, and tartan bow ties matching tuxedo cummerbunds or complementing jewel-toned jackets. In the Mod era of the 1960s, the bow tie grew oversized, in wild colors. In the 1970s, chunky, rent-a-tux clip-on bow ties entered the formal arena, but adjusted back to classic and tiny in the 1980s. By the end of the twentieth century, both black tie and white tie retained aficionados, but the necktie increasingly replaced bow ties at ceremonial events.

In the contemporary era, acceptance by fashionistas, sports figures, and celebrities has led to a redefinition of the bow tie, no longer limiting the accessory to weddings and senior proms, and classic styles have exploded in experimental patterns and colors. Confidence is crucial to rocking the modern bow tie, which is best carelessly hand-knotted to avoid an uptight appearance.

A tasteful bow tie indicates an individual who waltzes to his own melody, and who recognizes that this moment in the knotted accessory's story is the next stage in the progression of a thrilling fashion tradition.

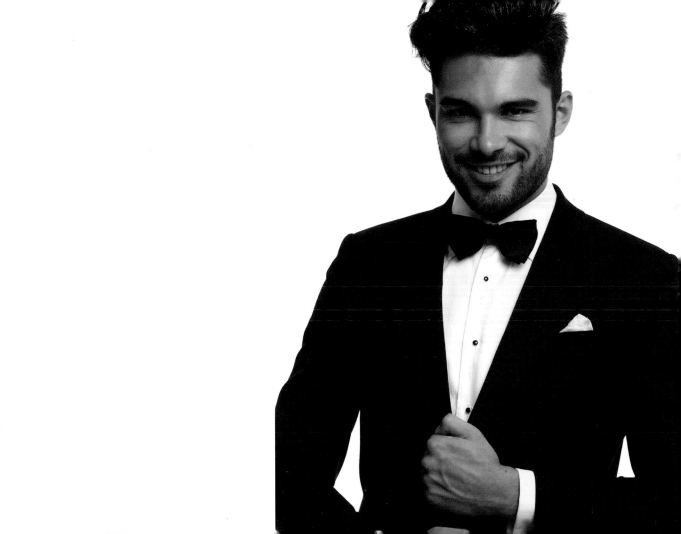

Gee, If I'd known I was going to get my picture taken

I would have worn a bow tie.

—Archibald Cox

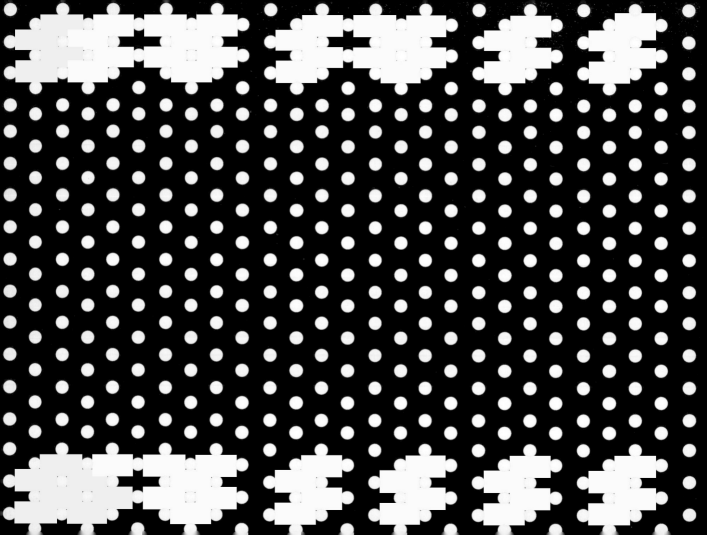

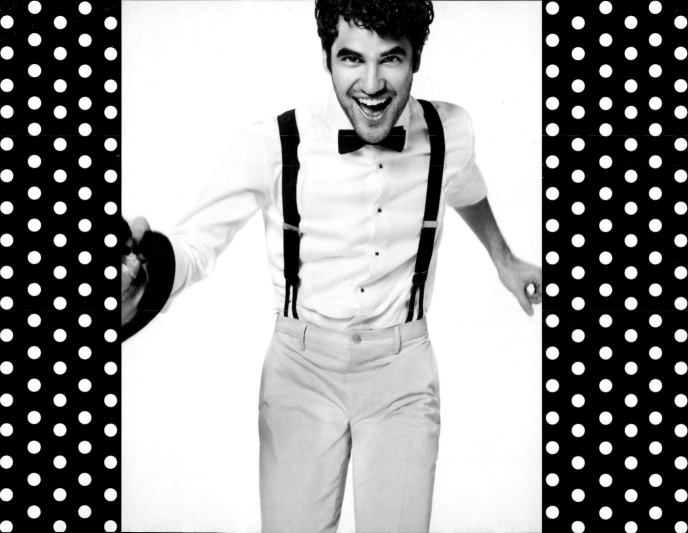

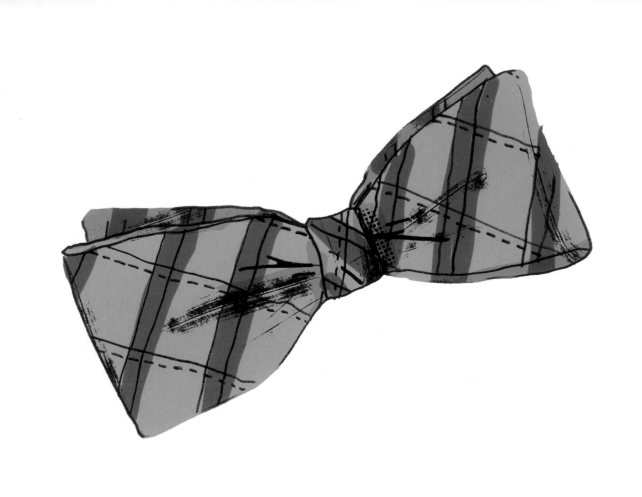

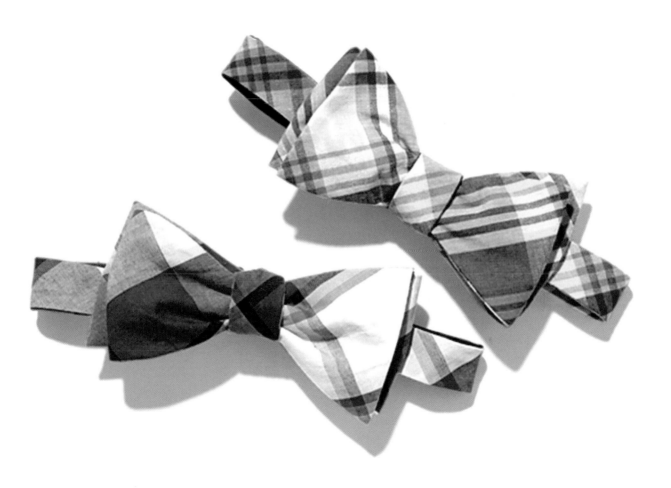

A man that refuses to wear a bow tie is a man that is afraid to experiment. A man that is afraid to experiment is no man at all.

—Christopher Callis, *Esquire*

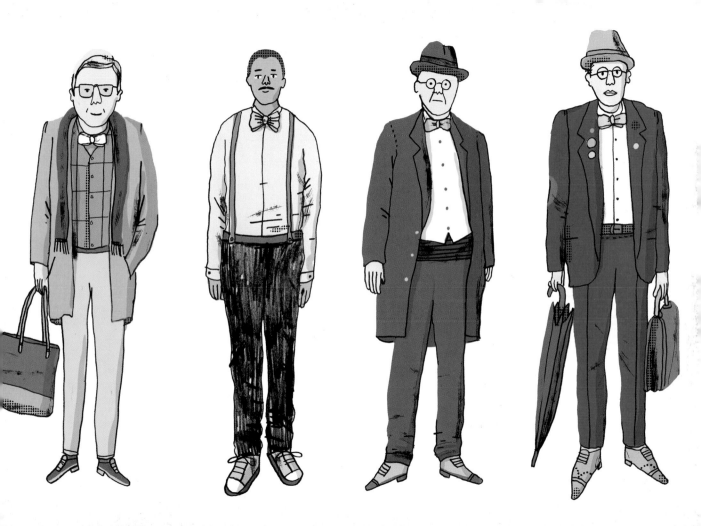

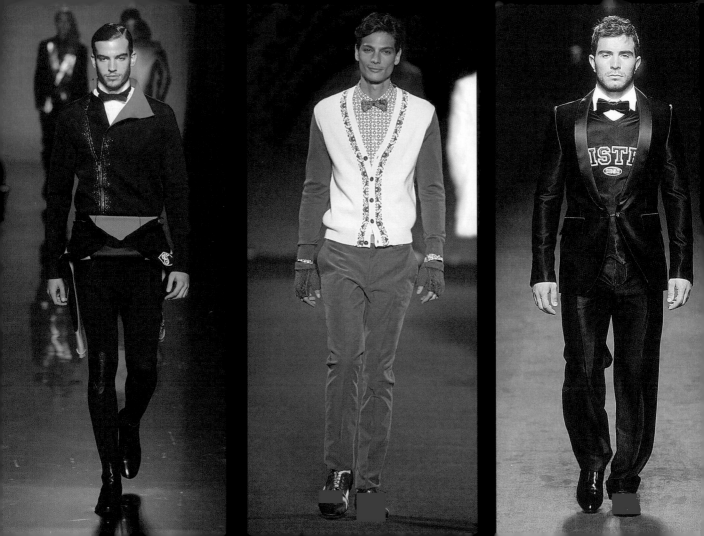

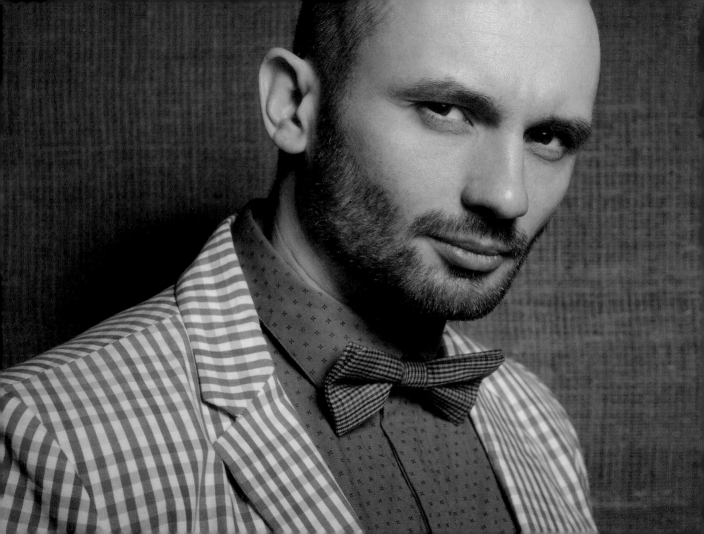

When you wear a bow tie, you have to turn off the part of the brain that cares about other people's perceptions.

—Tucker Carlson, *The New York Times*

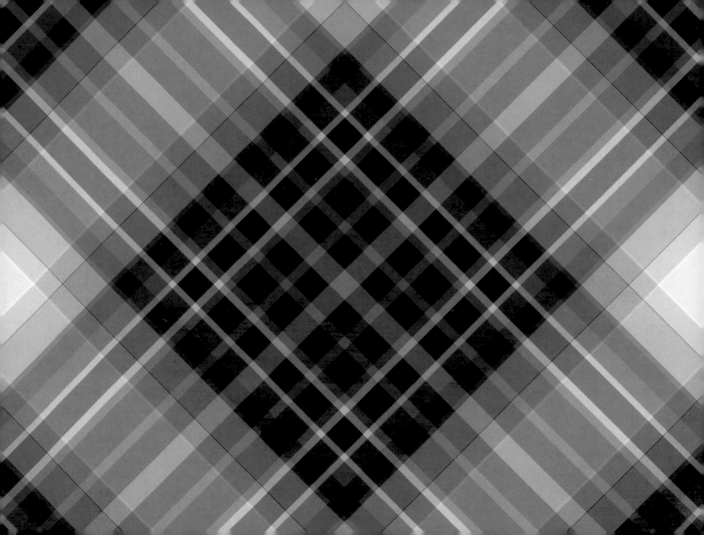

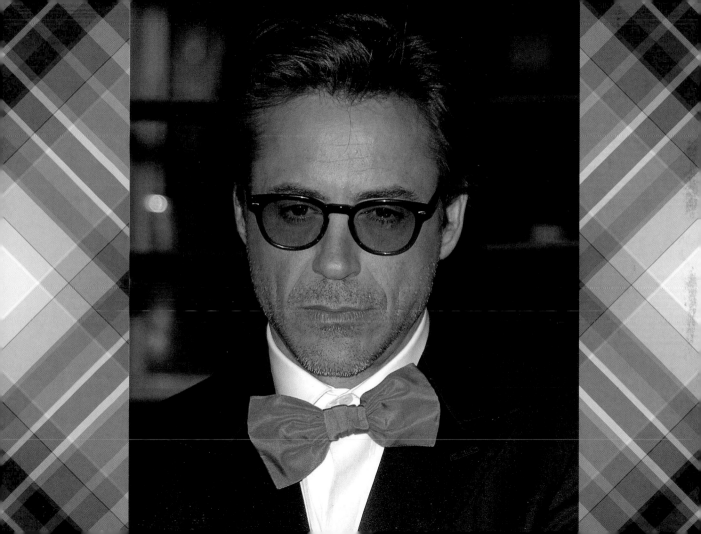

When people know this is a bow tie that the person wearing it has tied, I think it raises the bar from a fashion statement to a personal achievement.

—Don Owen

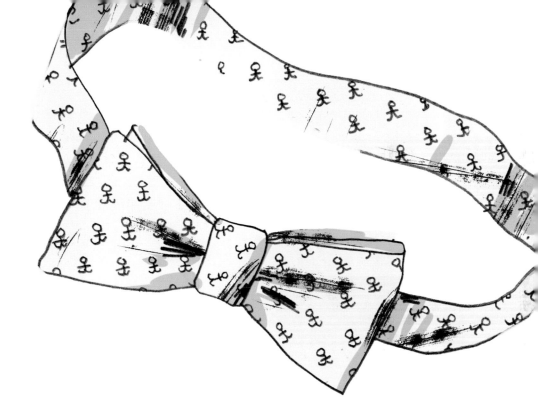

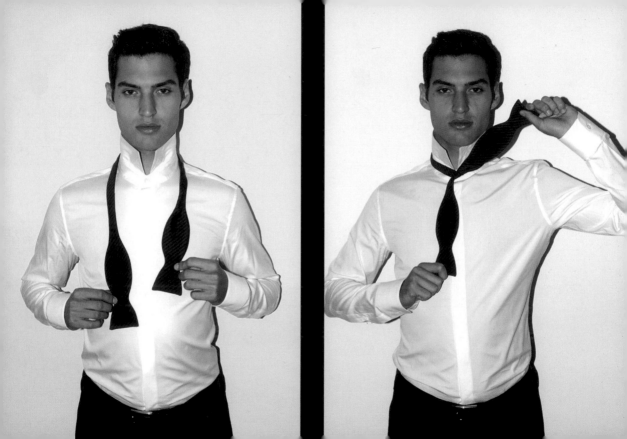

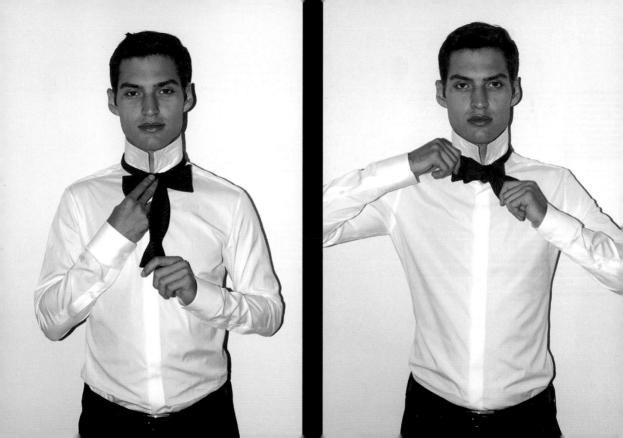

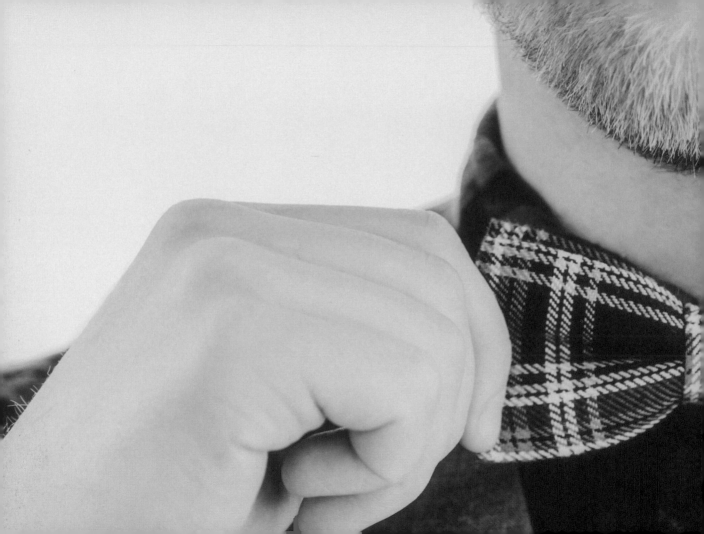

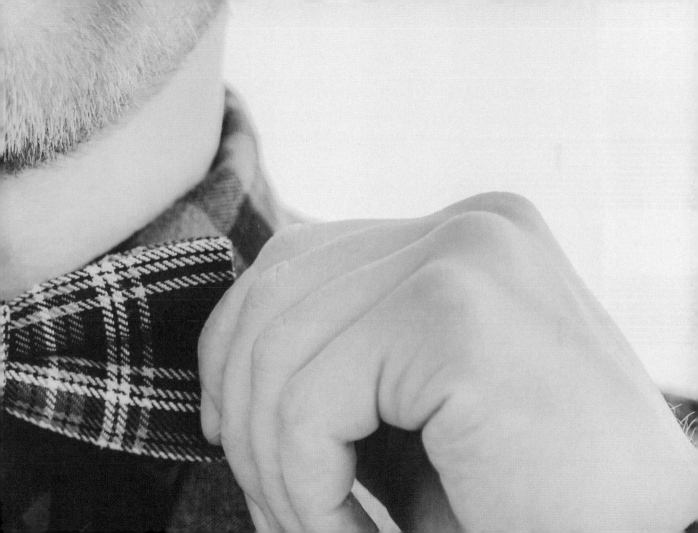

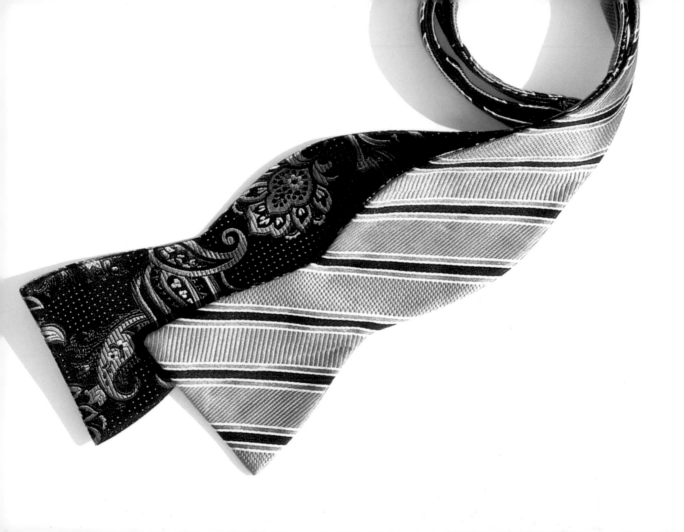

When you wear a bow tie, doors open for you. Your posture is a little more erect; your shoulders are a little farther back; your style is a little more dynamic. It's about the reestablishment of the gentleman.

—Dhani Jones

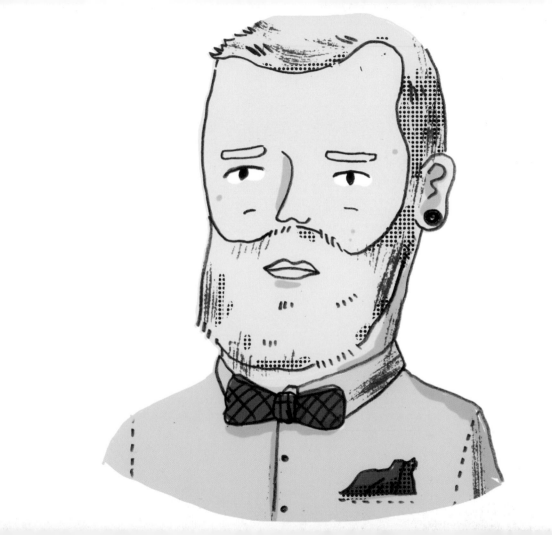

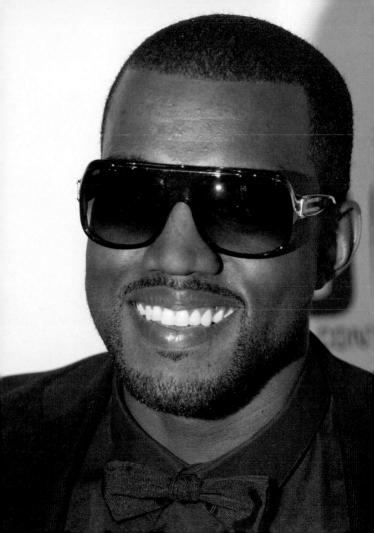

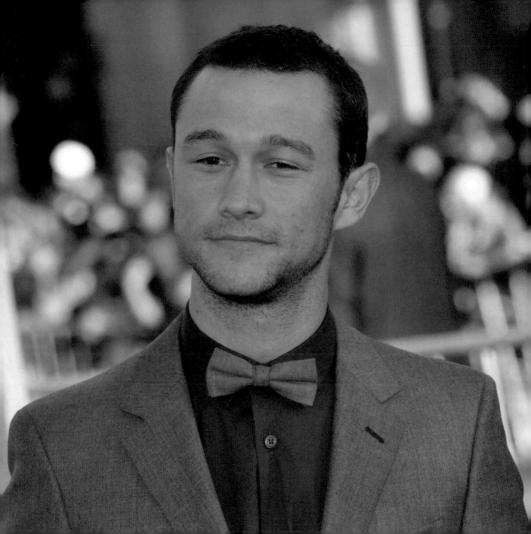

*T*he key to pulling off a bow tie is putting it on in the first place. Doing so demonstrates a playful, defiant sort of confidence. The goal is to make it look effortless.

—Andy Stager, co-founder of
The Cordial Churchman bow-tie company

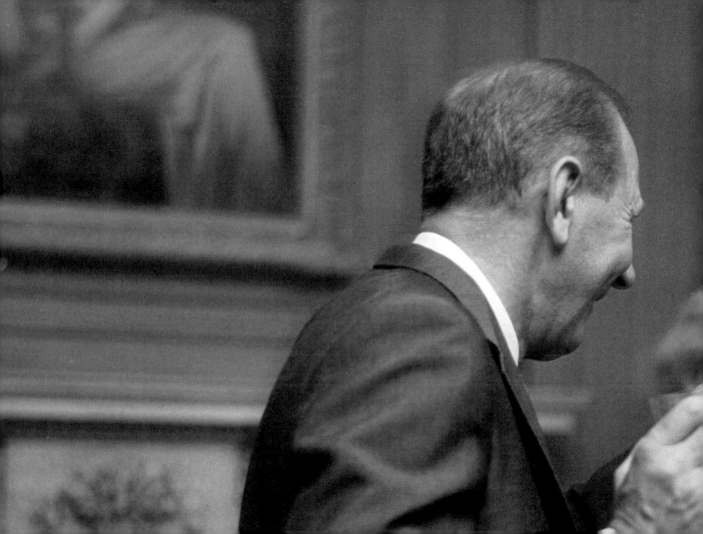

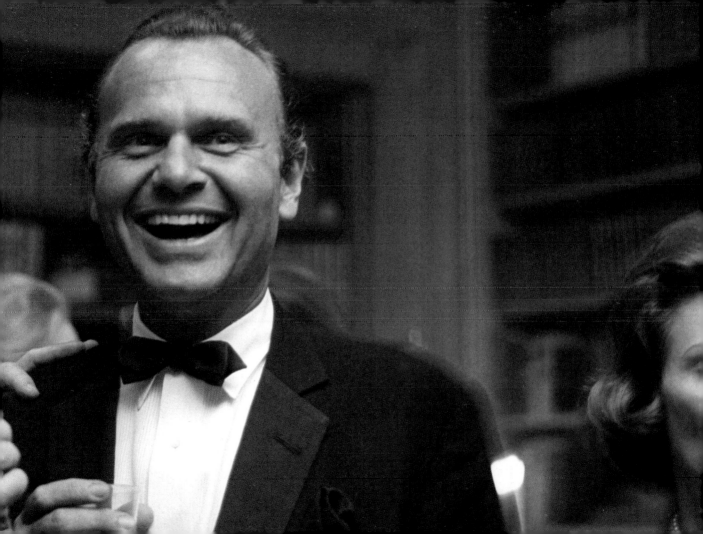

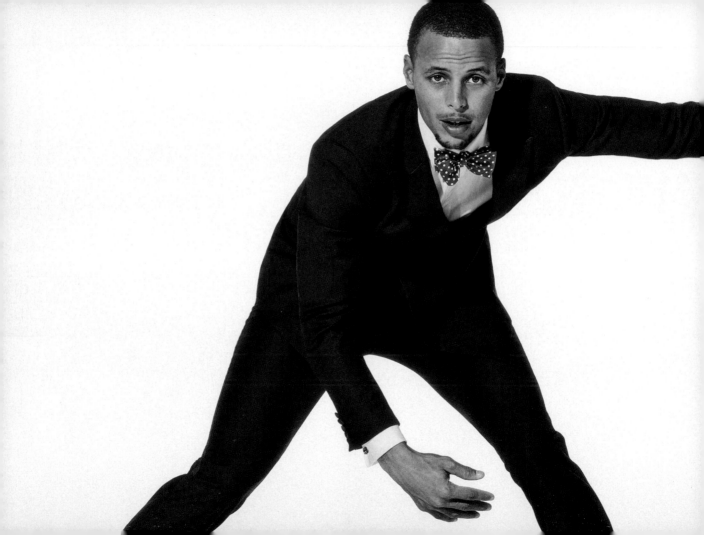

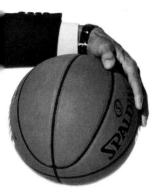

Mo's Bows is a company I started in Memphis, Tennessee, in 2011 when I was just nine years old. I couldn't find fun and cool bow ties, so one day I decided to use my Granny's scrap fabric to make and sell my own. I like to wear bow ties because they make me look good and feel good. Designing a colorful bow tie is just part of my vision to make the world a fun and happier place.

—Moziah Bridges, twelve-year-old entrepreneur, creator of Mo's Bows

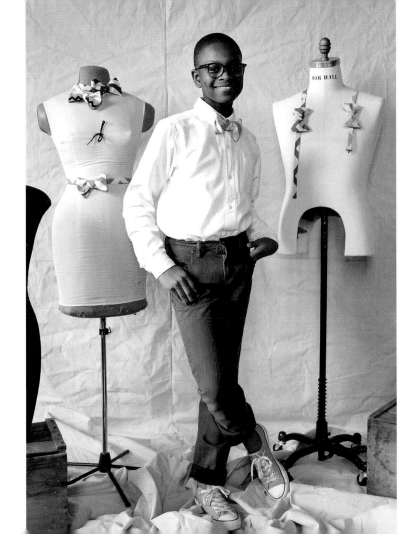

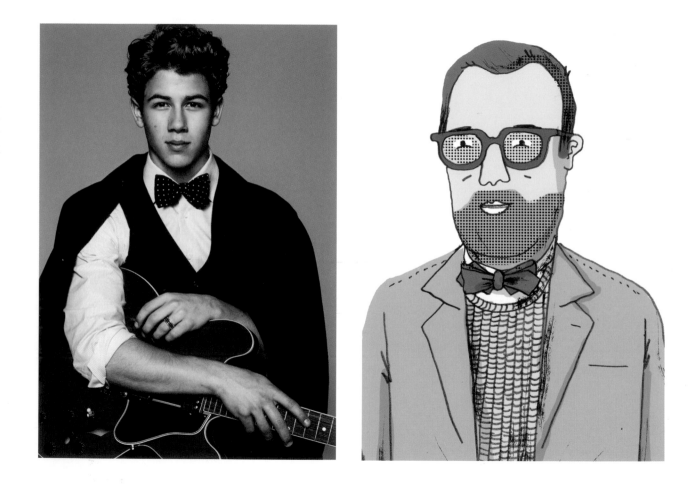

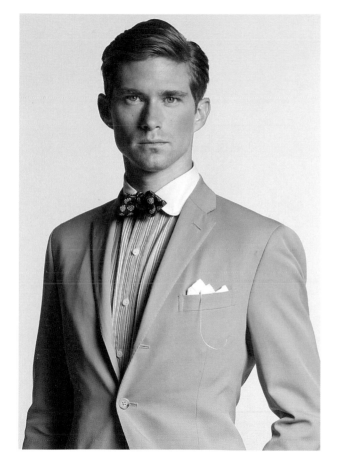
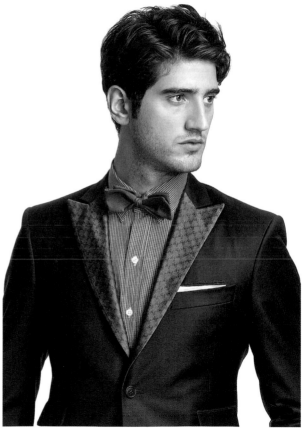

*T*he last thing I bought and loved was a selection of silk bow ties from Charvet, one of those wonderfully old-fashioned places of which there are now so few. I almost always wear a bow tie.

—Manolo Blahnik

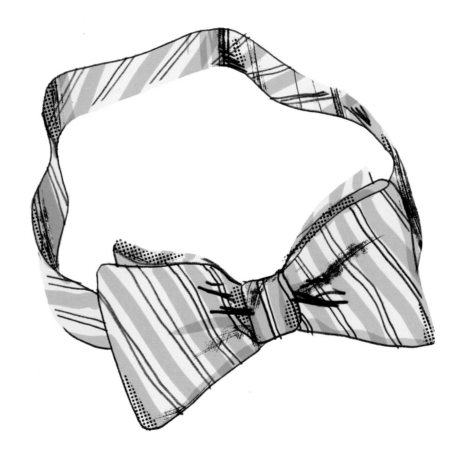

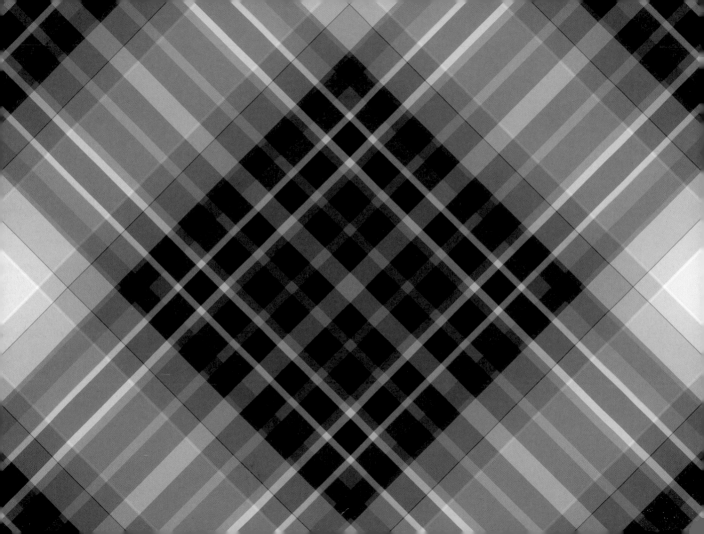

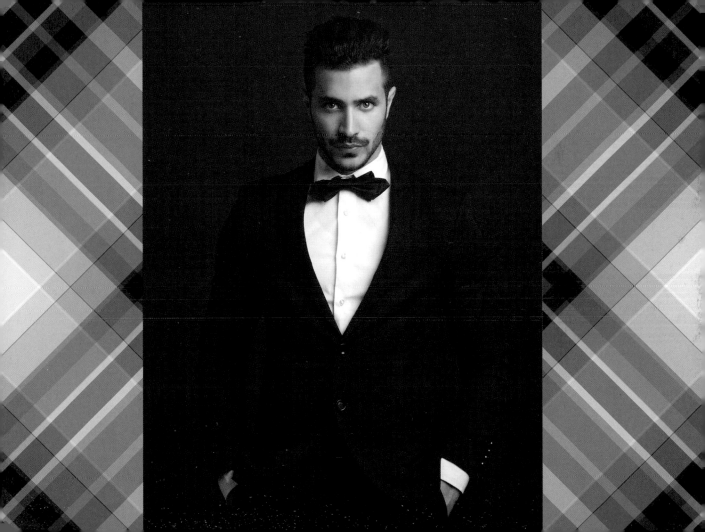

If you tie your own bow tie and it's a little floppy or off-kilter, don't sweat it. It's not supposed to look perfect; it's supposed to look real.

—"How to Pull Off a Bow Tie," *GQ*

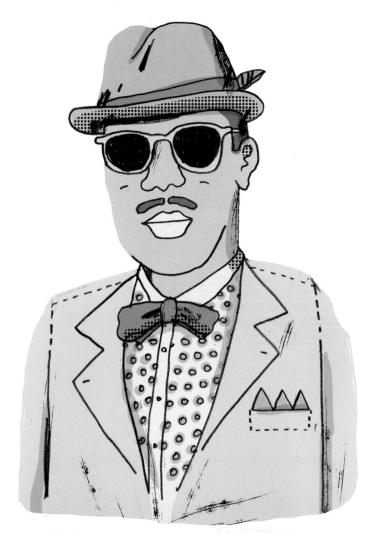

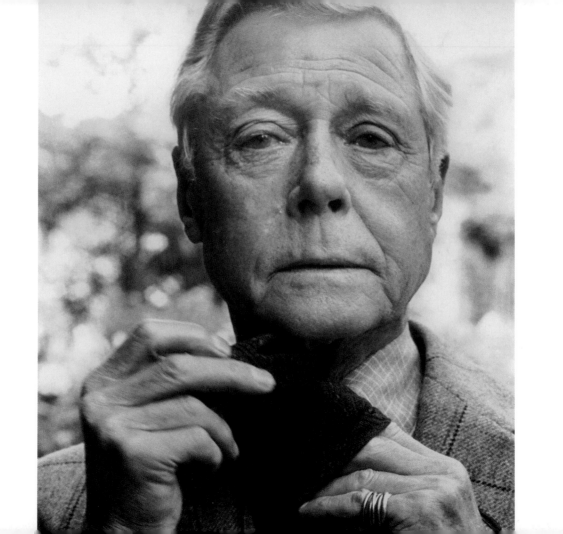

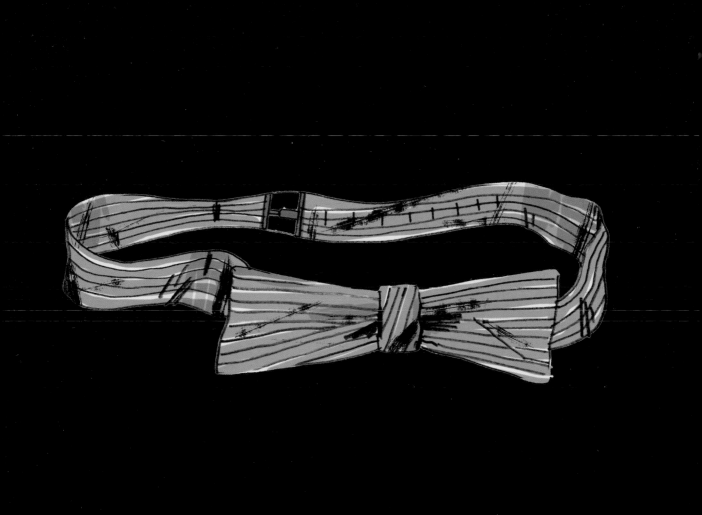

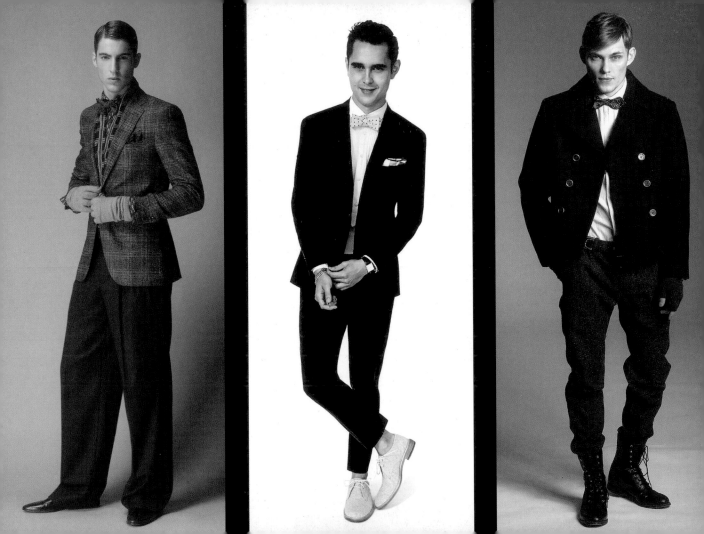

My father was a very good Boy Scout. He was very skilled with knots, and he showed me how to tie a bow tie.

—Bill Nye, scientist, television host

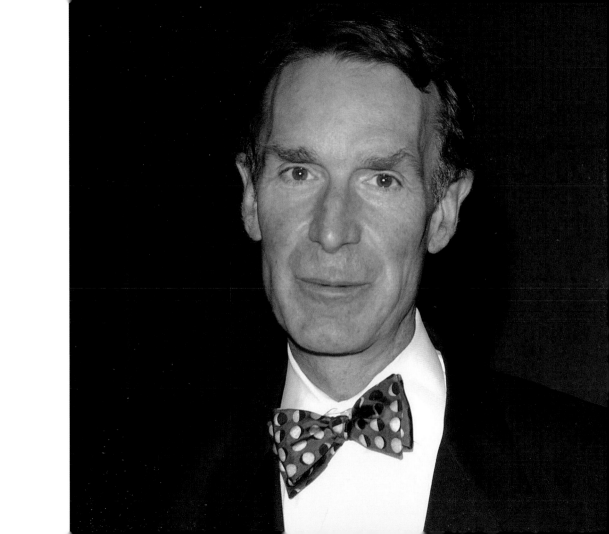

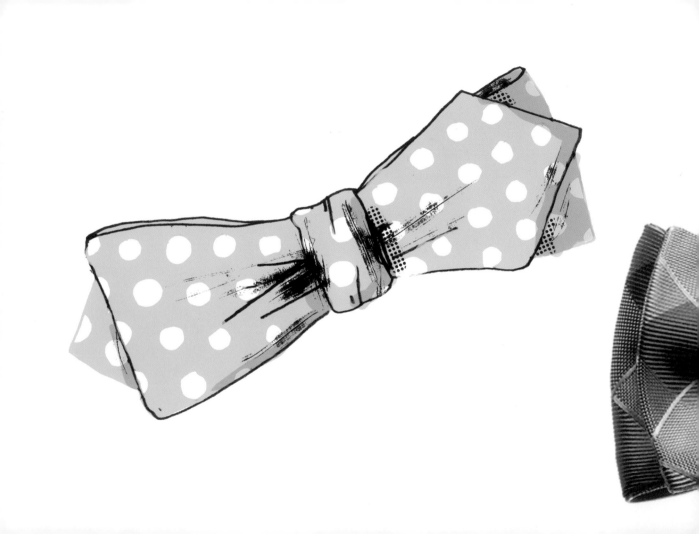

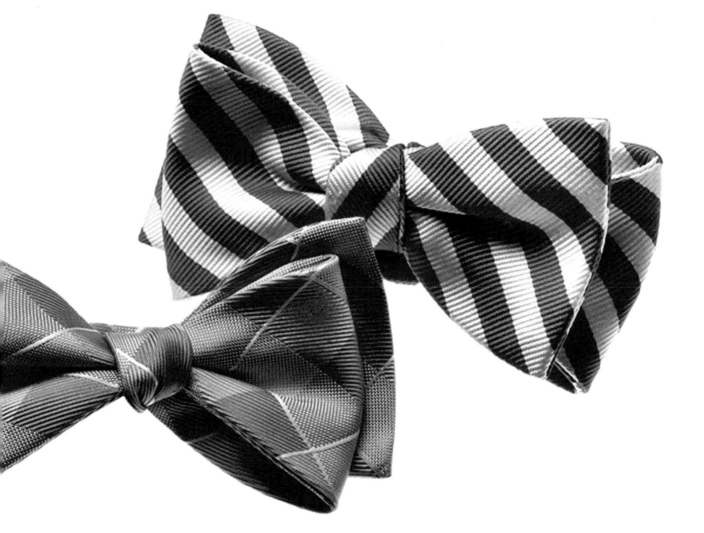

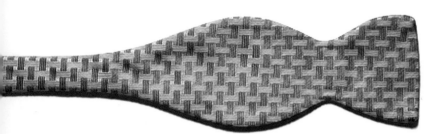

*B*ow ties are tricky.

They carry strong connotations: conservative, newspaperman, high-school principal. They are instant signs of nerddom in Hollywood movies. They look fastidious but not exactly sexy. I like them.

—Russell Smith, "Rock the Bow Tie without Looking Nerdy," *The Globe and Mail*

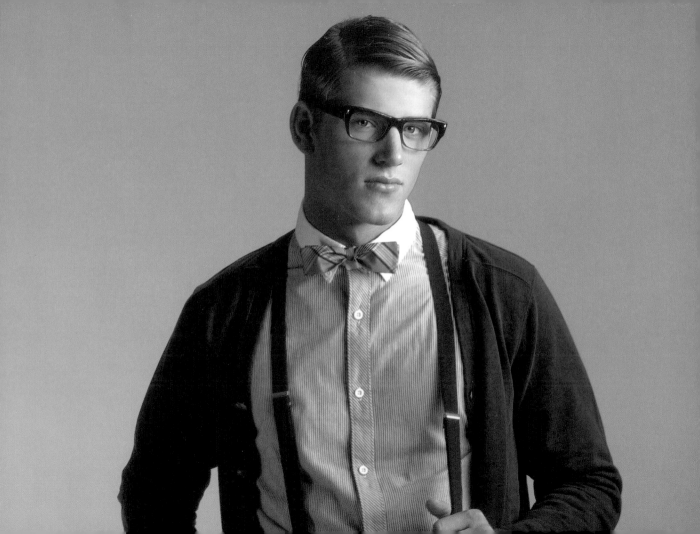

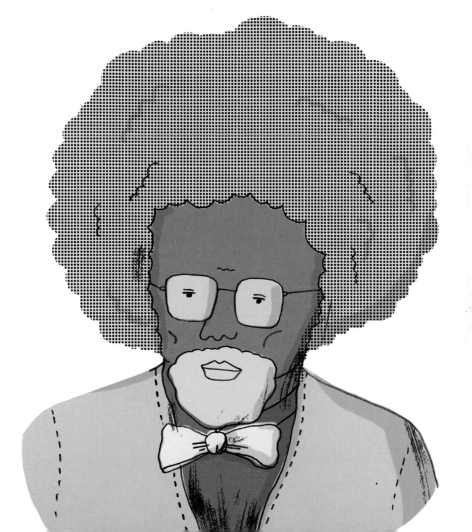

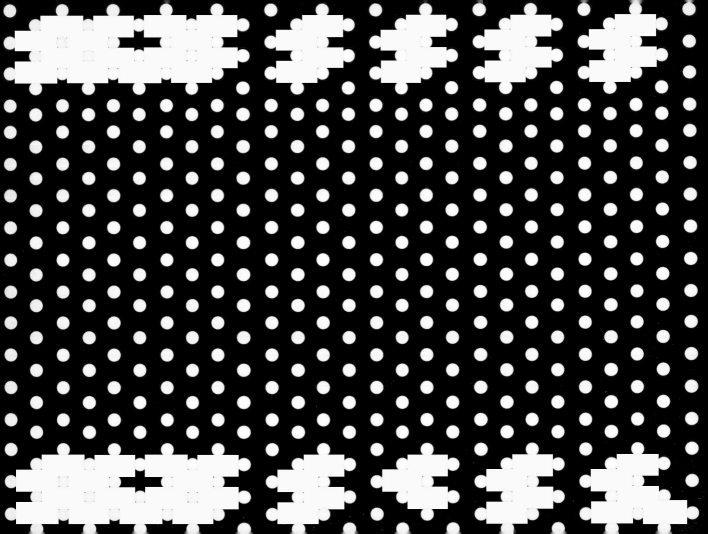

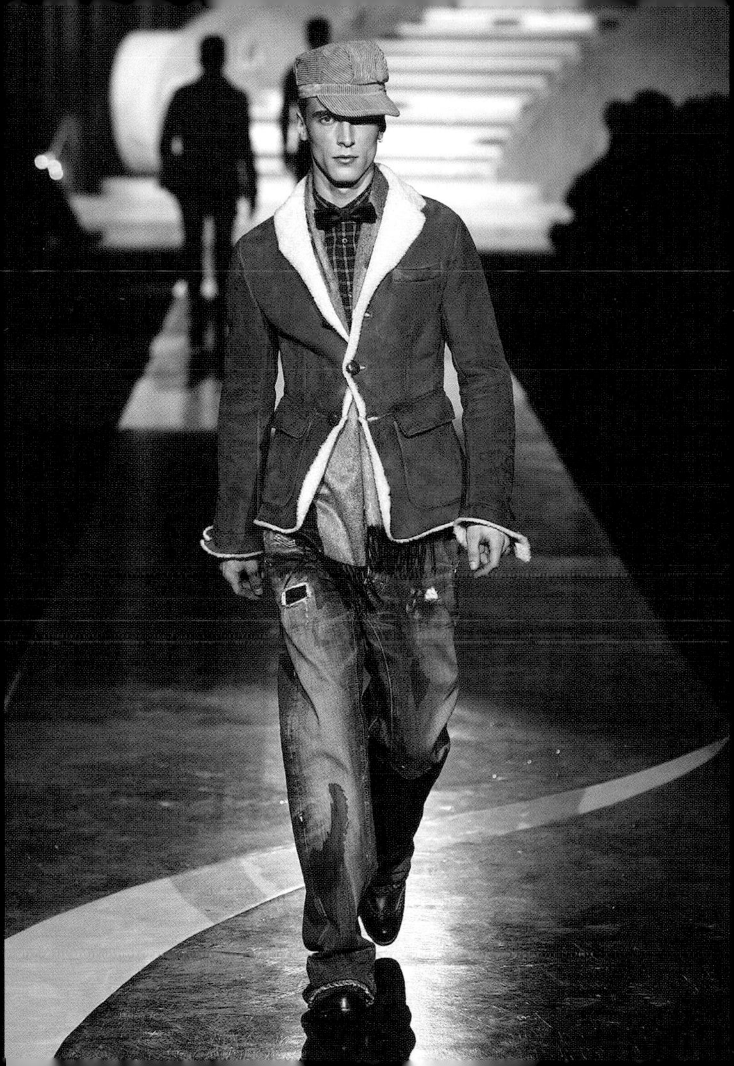

There is a certain responsibility associated with wearing a bow tie, so I always tell folks to wear it well and behave like a gentleman.

—James Hill, co-owner of High Cotton Ties

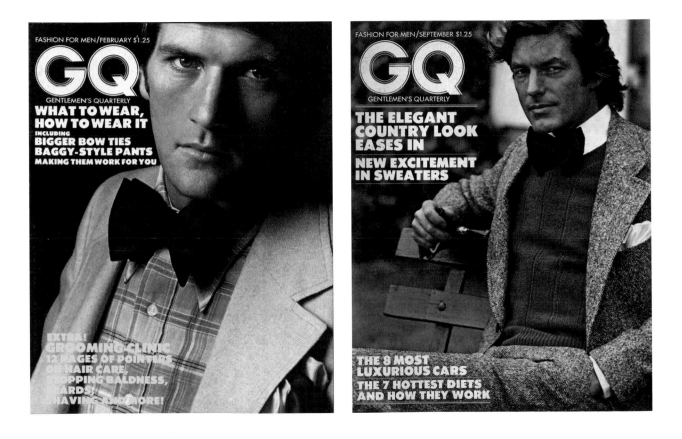

FASHION FOR MEN/FEBRUARY $1.25

GQ
GENTLEMEN'S QUARTERLY

WHAT TO WEAR, HOW TO WEAR IT
INCLUDING
BIGGER BOW TIES
BAGGY-STYLE PANTS
MAKING THEM WORK FOR YOU

EXTRA!
GROOMING CLINIC
12 PAGES OF POINTERS
ON HAIR CARE,
STOPPING BALDNESS,
BEARDS,
SHAVING AND MORE!

FASHION FOR MEN/SEPTEMBER $1.25

GQ
GENTLEMEN'S QUARTERLY

THE ELEGANT COUNTRY LOOK EASES IN
NEW EXCITEMENT IN SWEATERS

THE 8 MOST LUXURIOUS CARS
THE 7 HOTTEST DIETS AND HOW THEY WORK

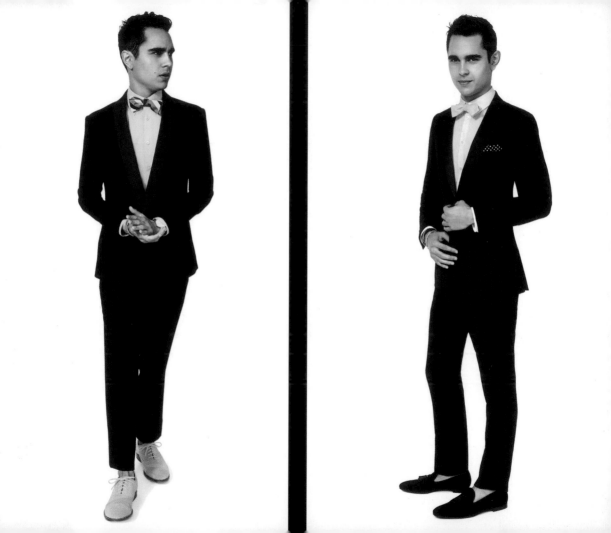

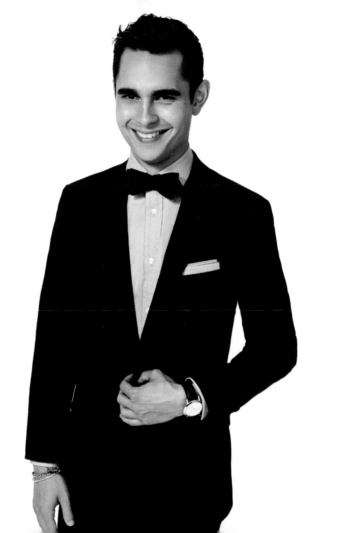

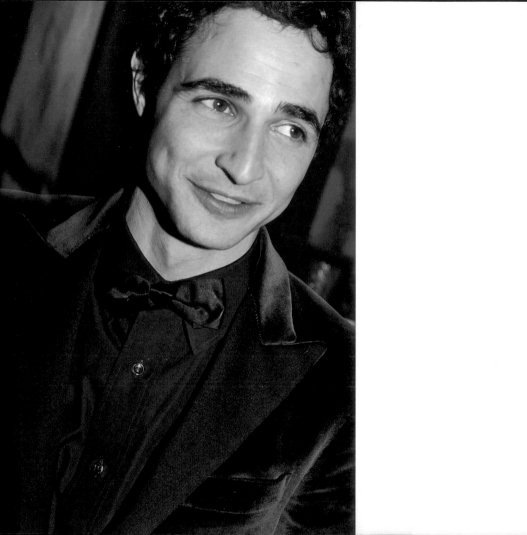

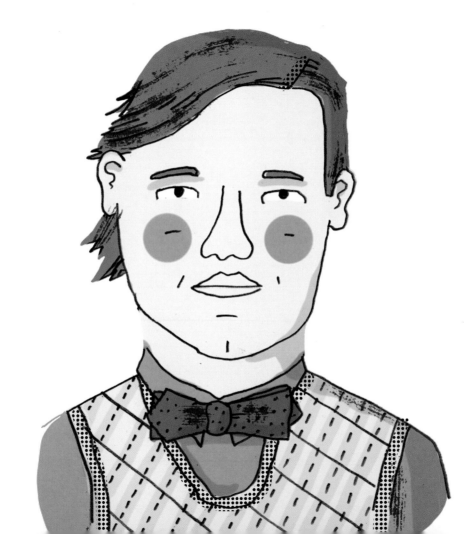

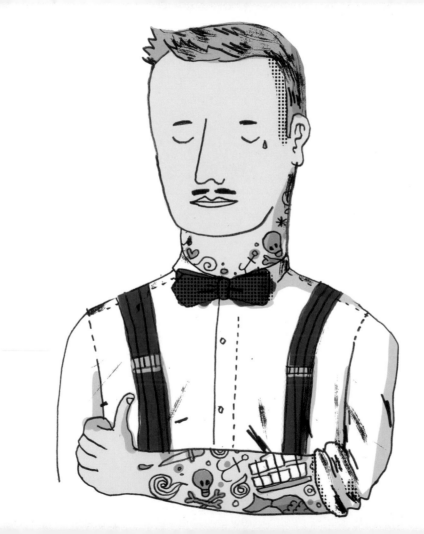

*A*n interesting fact of public perception is that if you wear one three times a year, then you are considered a bow-tie wearer.

—George Will, *The New York Times*

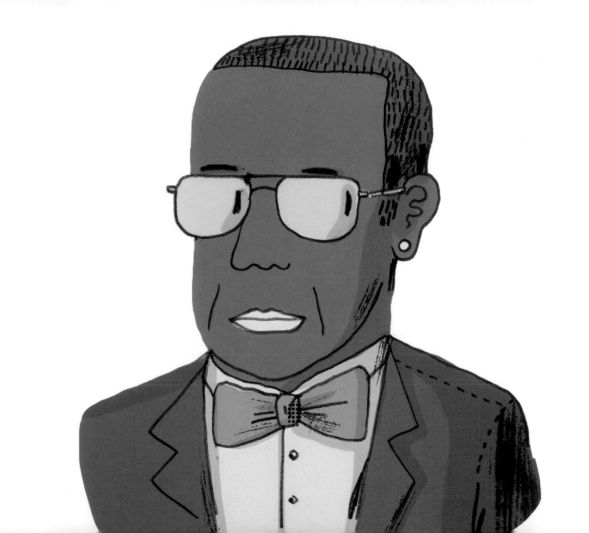

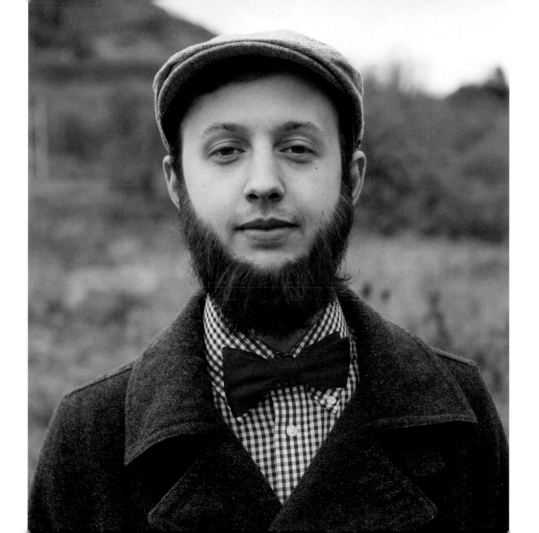

And you're wearing a bow tie.
See my point?

Now, I'm not saying you're not a smart man, because those are hard to tie.

—Jon Stewart to Tucker Carlson

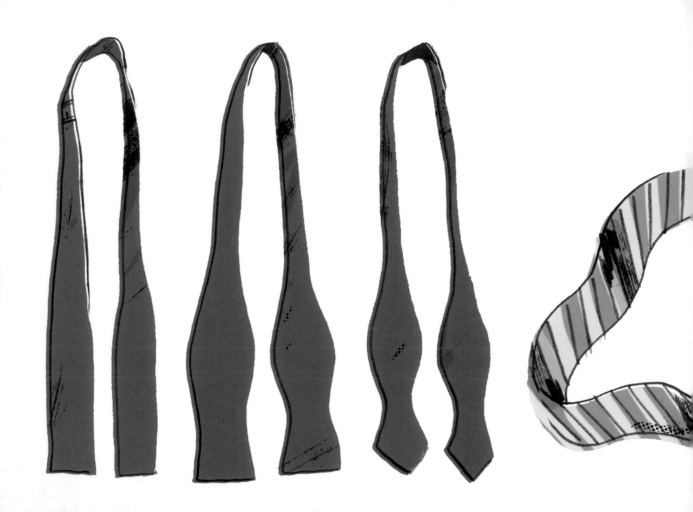

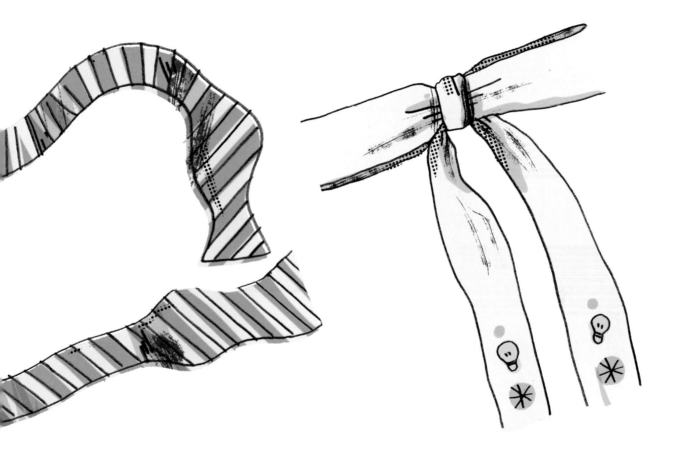

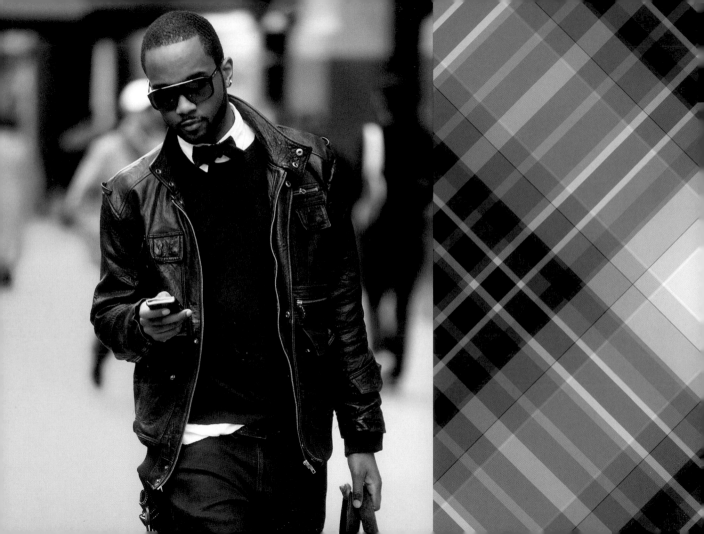

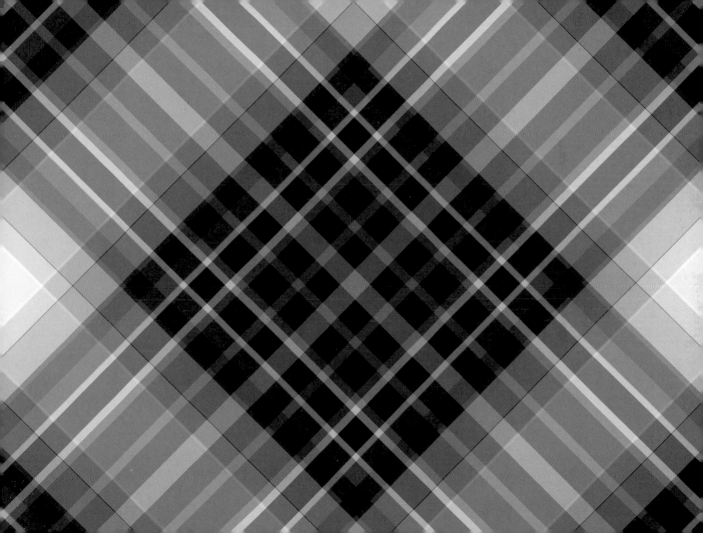

Whenever I wear one, women smile.

—K. Cooper Ray,
The Wall Street Journal

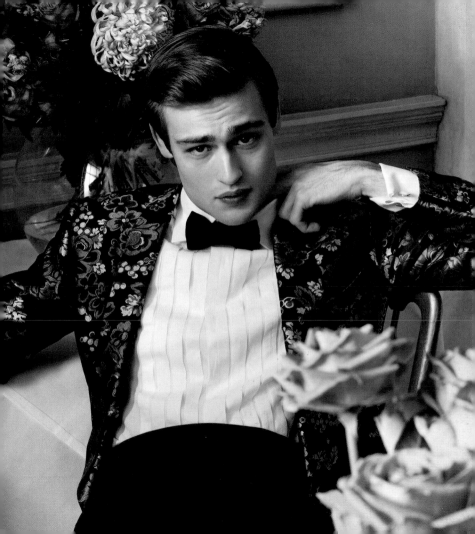

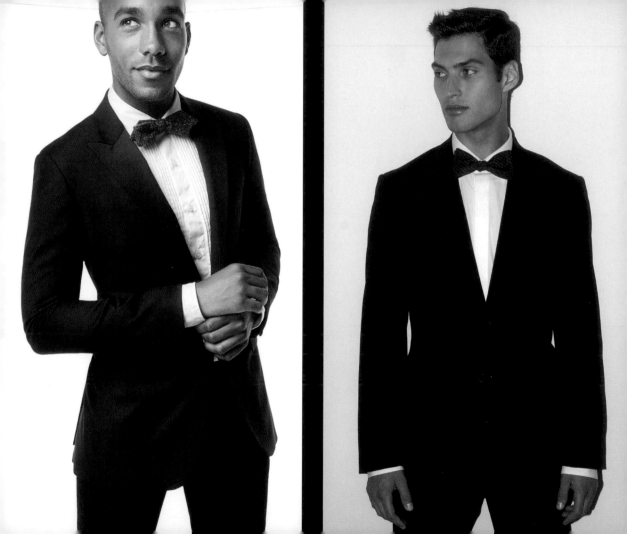

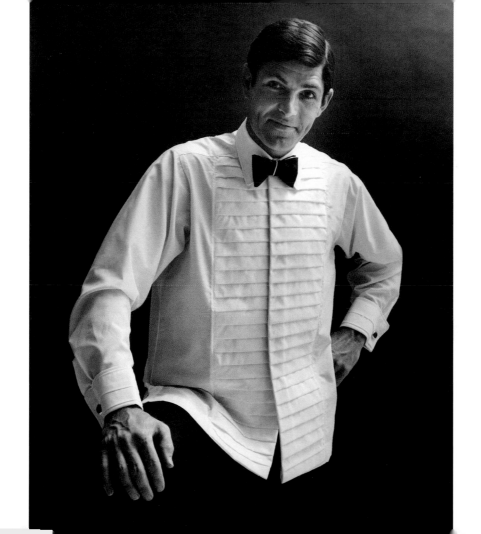

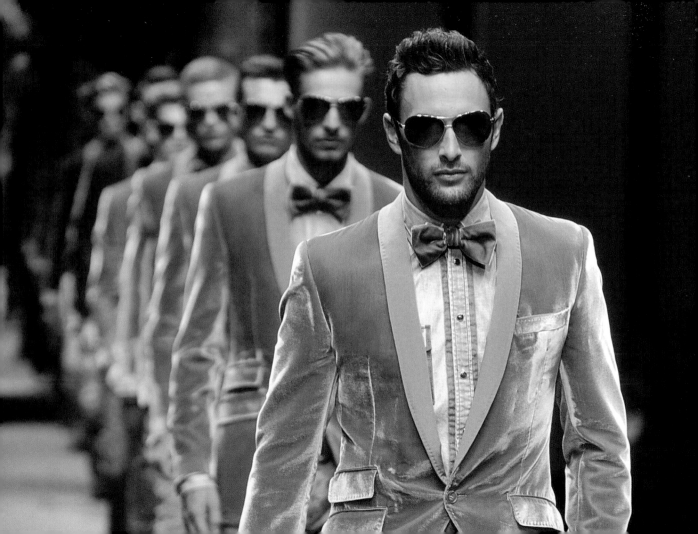

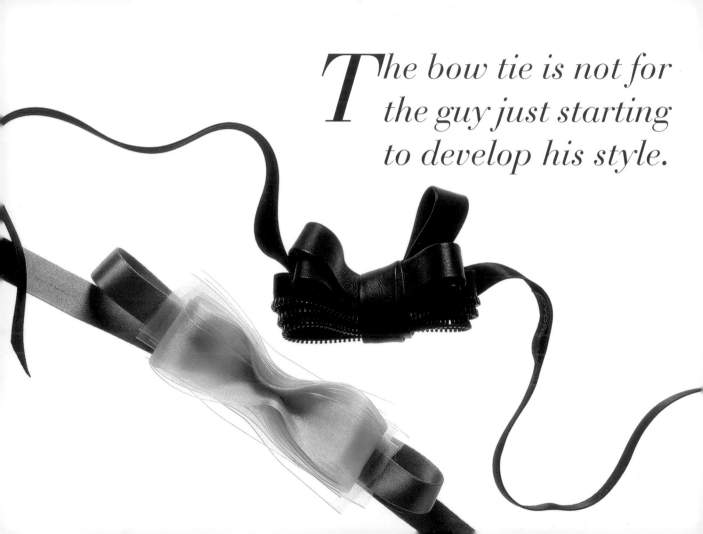

The bow tie is not for the guy just starting to develop his style.

Don't buy one before you understand the proportions of your clothes or before you've gotten a few straight ties first. But do buy a bow tie. Buy it when you have your basics down and are ready to develop your style.

—Christopher Callis, *Esquire*

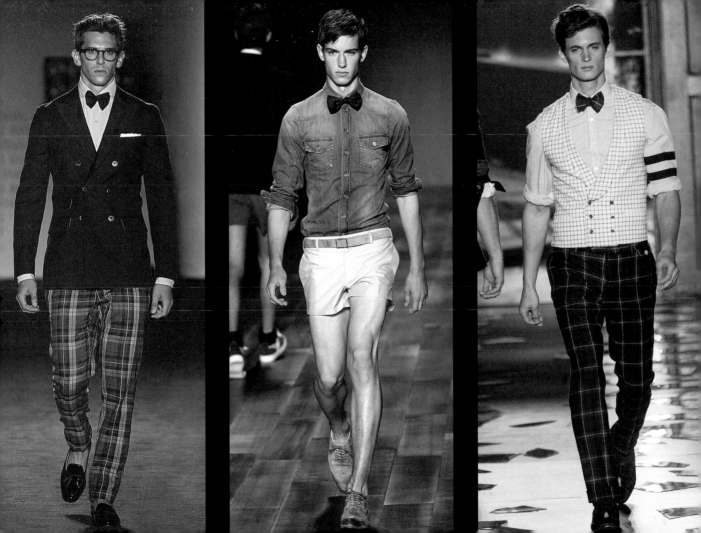

*B*ow ties are worn by magicians, country doctors, lawyers and professors and by people hoping to look like the above. But perhaps most of all, wearing a bow tie is a way of broadcasting an aggressive lack of concern for what other people think.

—Warren St. John, *The New York Times*

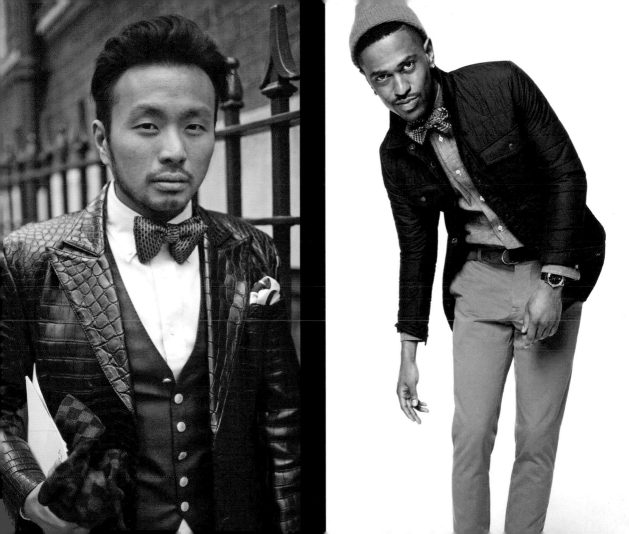

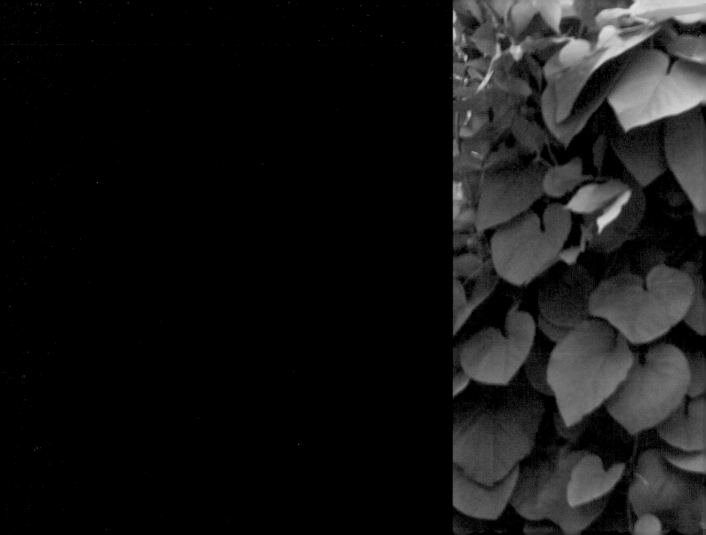

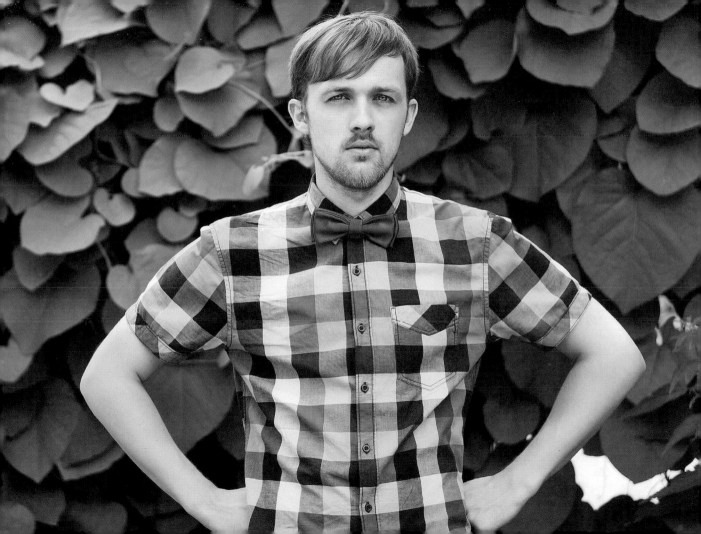

You can't dribble

on bow ties.

—Theodor "Dr. Seuss" Geisel

I love wearing bow ties for no particular reason.

—Brad Goreski

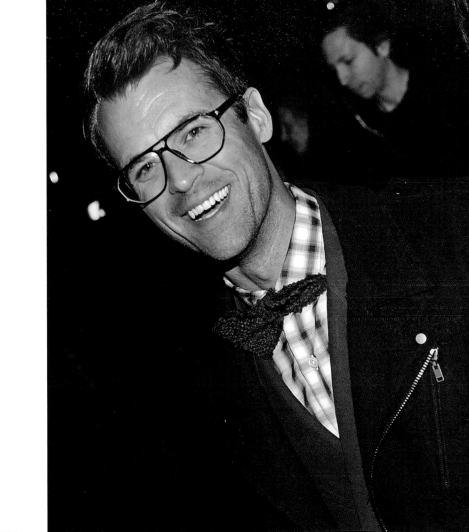

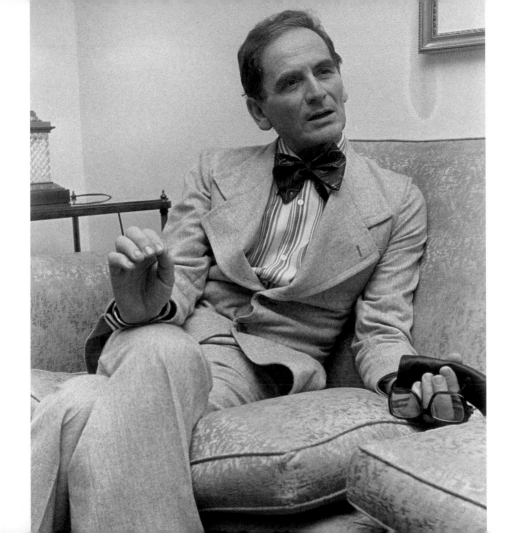

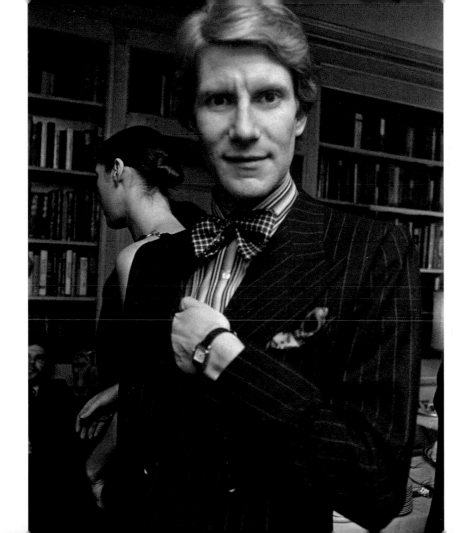

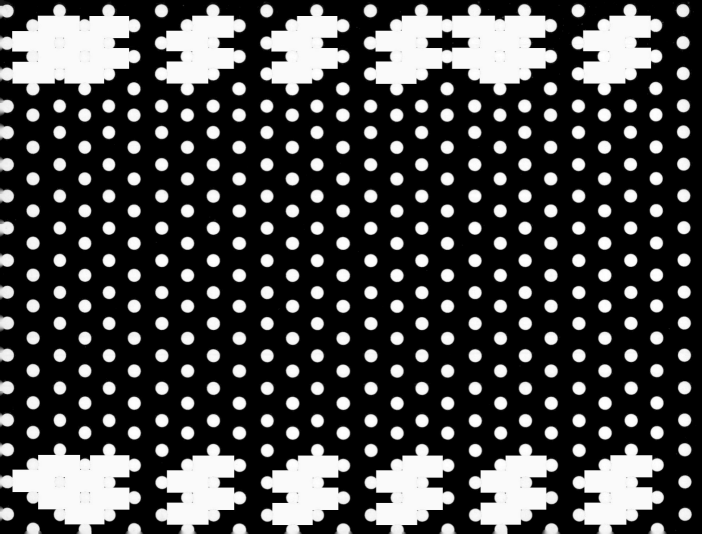

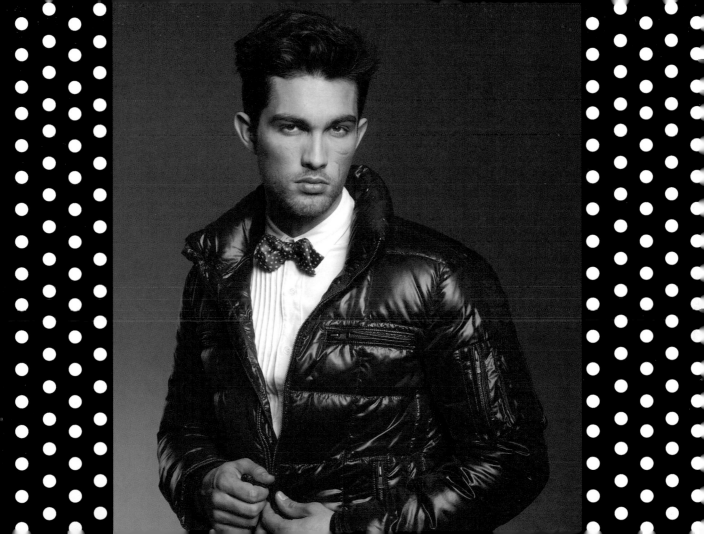

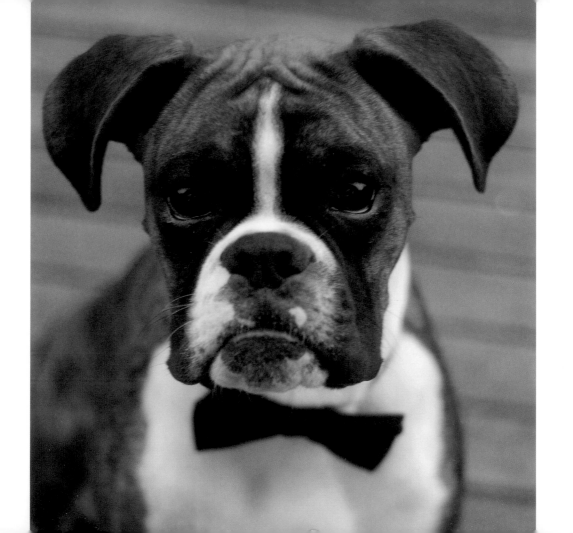

When [John Steinbeck] wasn't at home, he could be seen walking up and down Main Street—first with his French standard poodle, Charley, his companion during a 1960 road trip around the United States made by Mr. Steinbeck that became Travels with Charley: In Search of America, *which he also wrote while living in Sag Harbor.*

During one of his strolls, Mr. Steinbeck popped into [David] Lee's store once again after seeing his display window full of polka-dotted, patterned, colorful bow ties.

"Dave, I want a couple of those bow ties," Mr. Steinbeck said, his friend recalled.

"Sonny, you don't seem the bow tie type," Mr. Lee replied.

"No," Mr. Steinbeck agreed. "They're for Charley."

—Michelle Trauring, *The East Hampton Press*

Bow ties are cool.

—Doctor Who

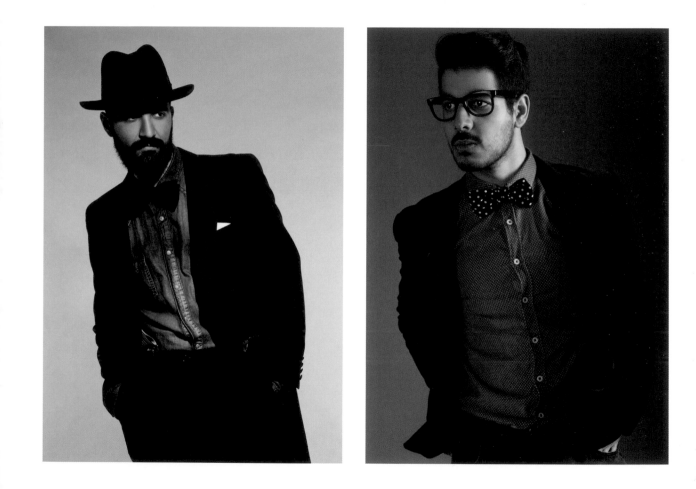

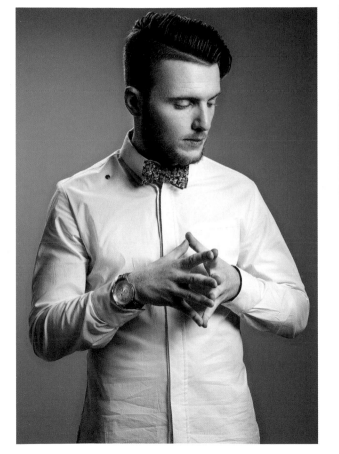
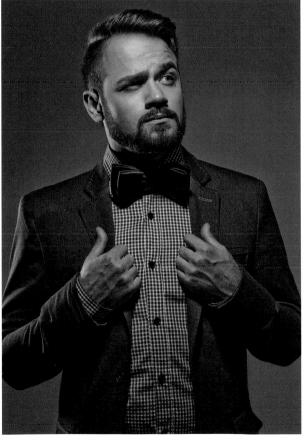

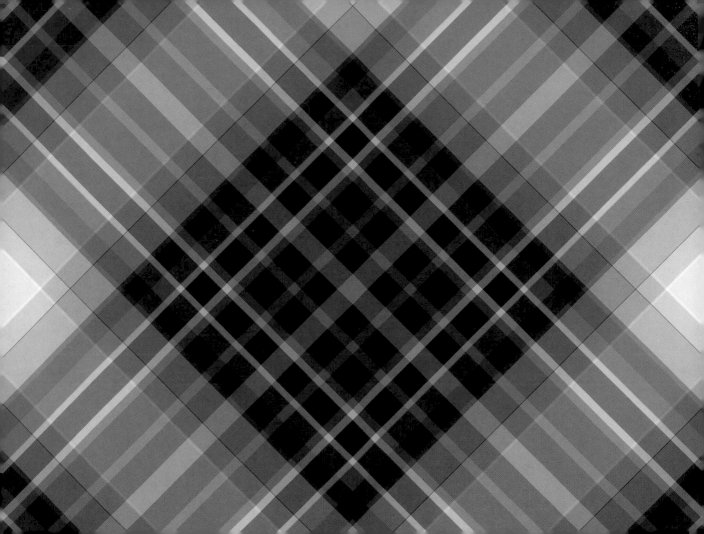

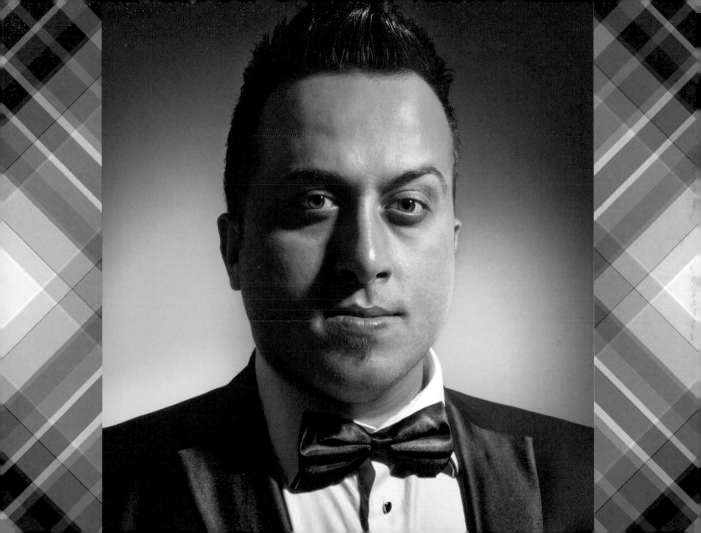

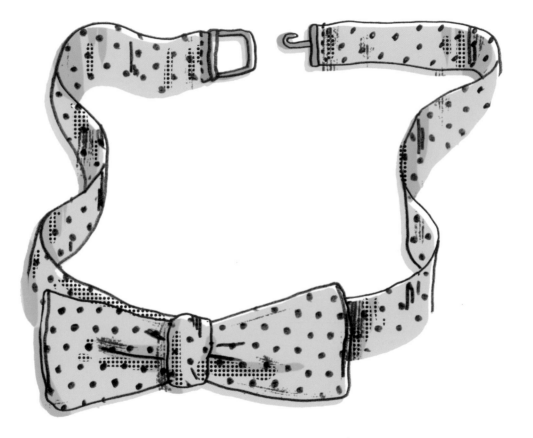

I like to think of a bow tie as a very charming man. He is witty, whimsical, and a bit eccentric. He has a few bad habits, such as smoking too many cigars, but his joie de vivre makes him memorable and captivating.

—Tanya Huang, founder and
designer at Knot Theory

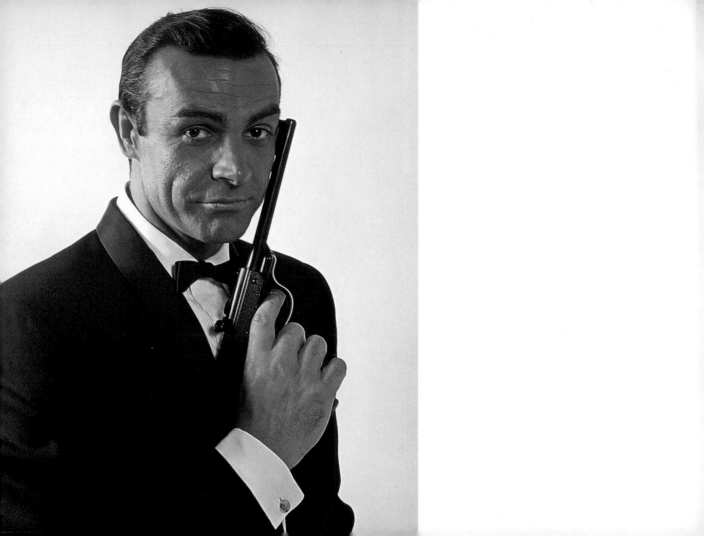

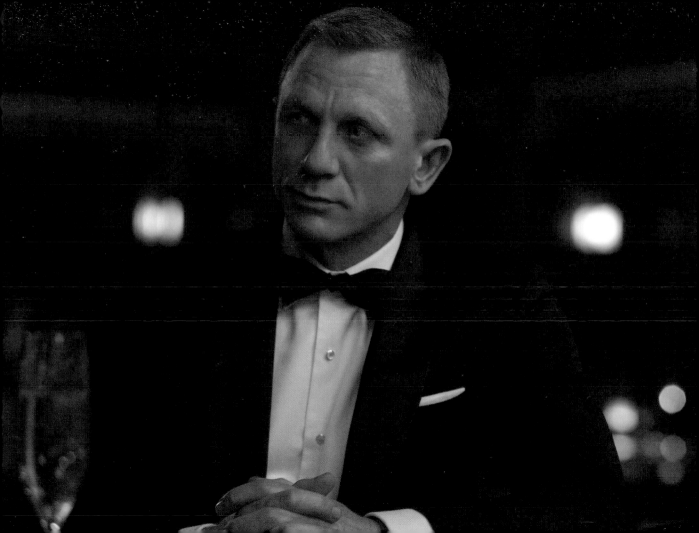

Moreover, the particular beauty of expressing your individuality by sporting a bow tie—as opposed to, say, wearing your pants backwards—is that the secret of your devilish non-mainstreamness will be perfectly obvious and instantly understood by everyone. No one can possibly misunderstand the message, and that's important. That way you can be certain that you'll inspire only the sort of disapproval that actually enhances your individualist credibility—even if, sometimes, you have to make up that disapproval yourself.

—Rob Walker, *Slate*

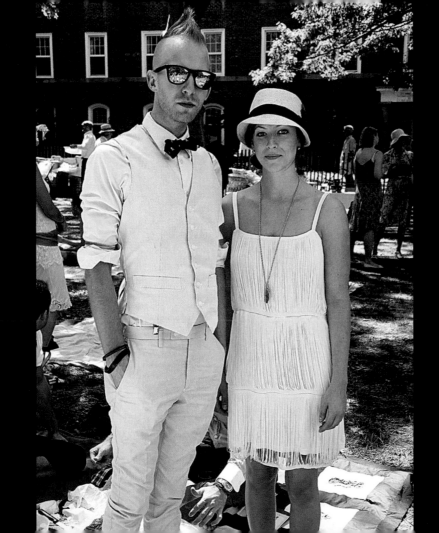

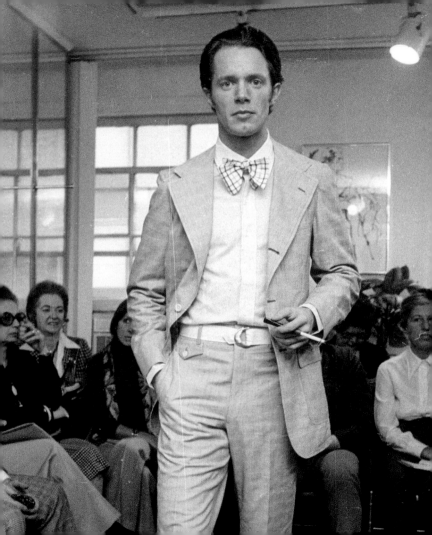

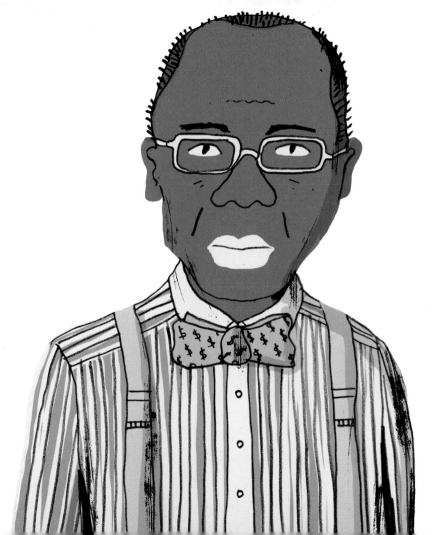

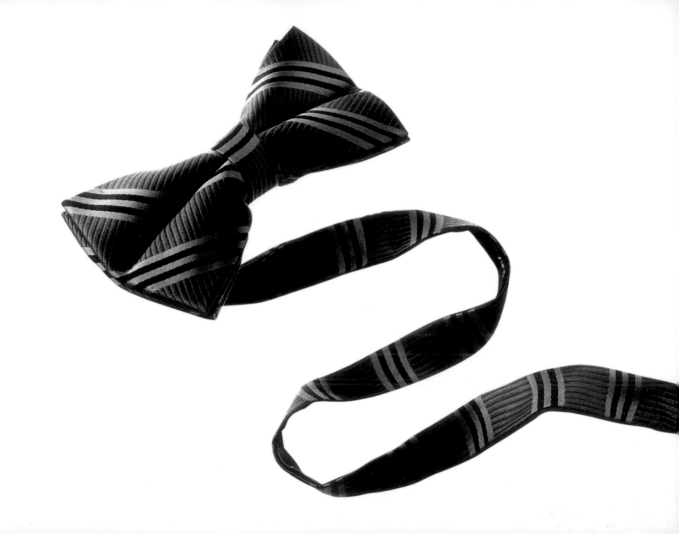

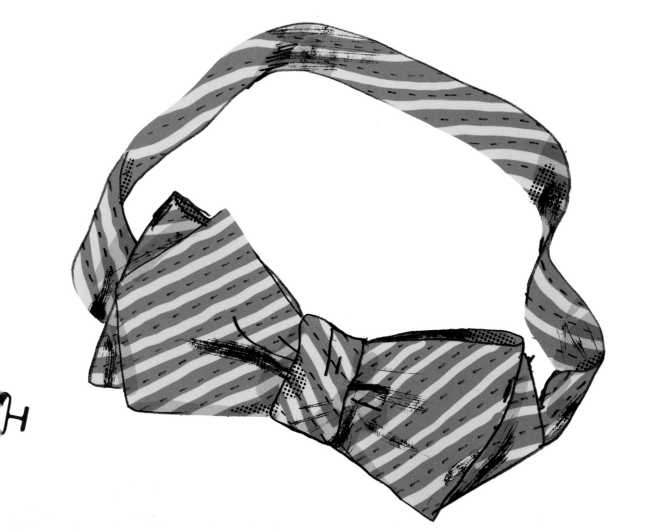

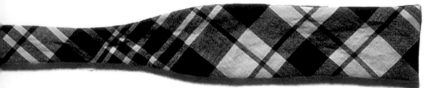

I *was a Laurel and Hardy nut.*

I got to know Laurel at the end of his life, and it was a great thrill for me. He left me his bow tie and derby and told me that if they ever made a movie about him, he'd want me to play him.

—Dick Van Dyke

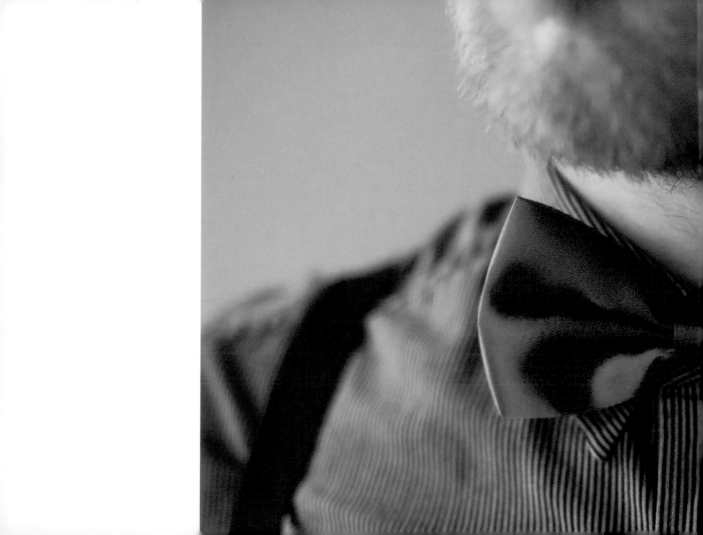

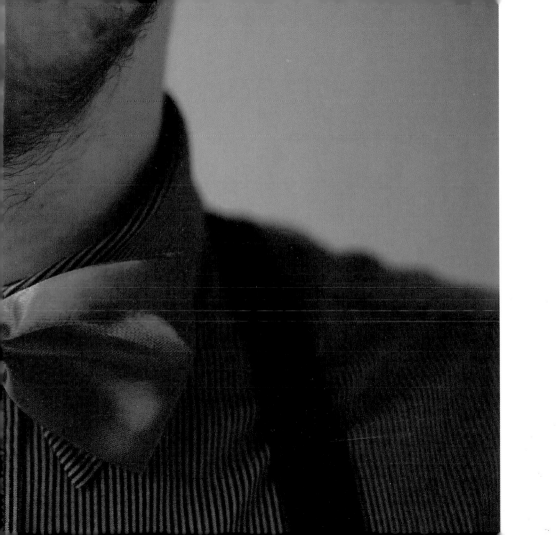

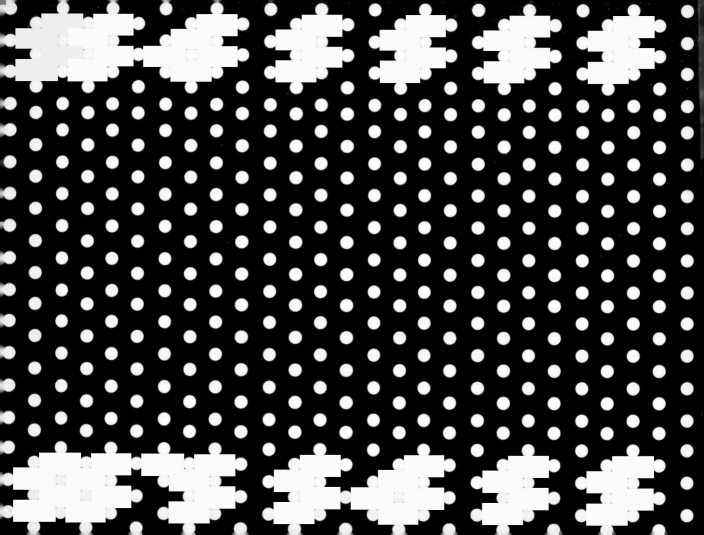

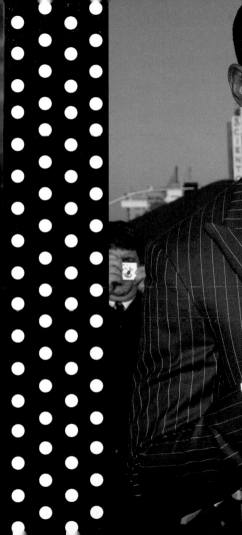

*T*he thing about a bow tie is that it does a lot of the talking for you. "Hey!" it shouts. "Look over here. I'm friendly, I'm interesting!"

—David Sedaris, "Buddy, Can You Spare a Tie?," *When You Are Engulfed in Flames*

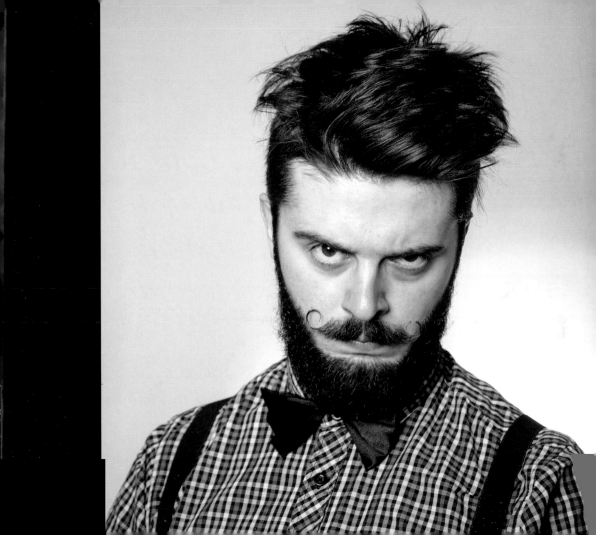

The Bow Tie Book

Published by Universe Publishing,
a division of Rizzoli International Publications, Inc.
300 Park Avenue South
New York, NY 10010
www.rizzoliusa.com

2014 2015 2016 2017 2018 / 10 9 8 7 6 5 4 3 2 1

Design by Kim Gatto

Printed in China
ISBN-13: 978-0-7893-2919-6
Library of Congress Call Number: 2014950292

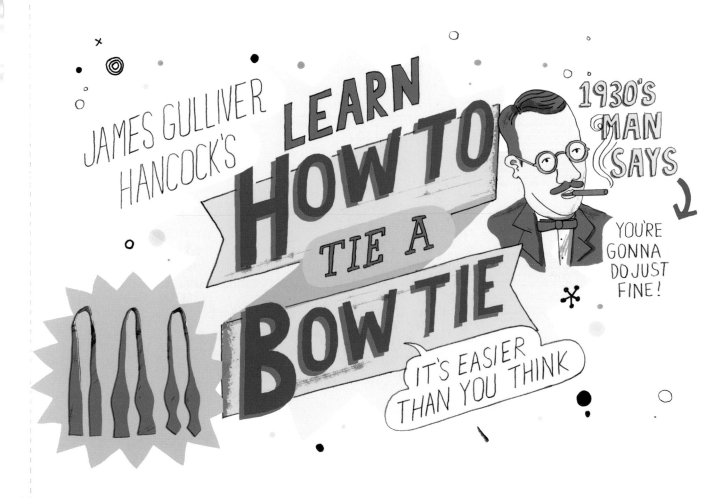

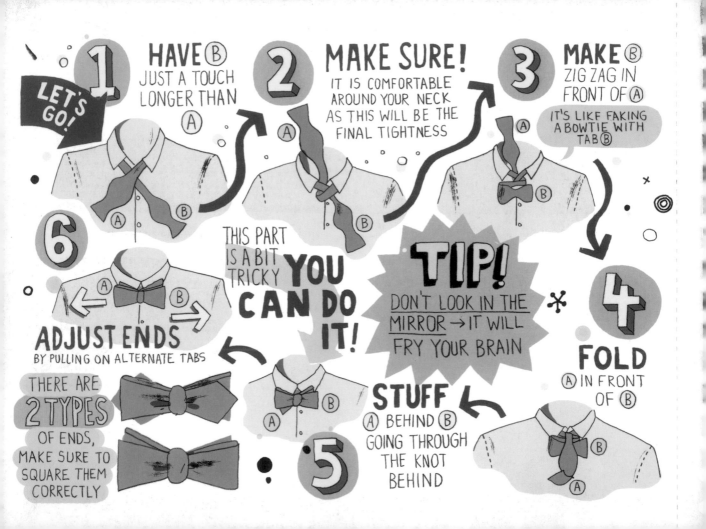

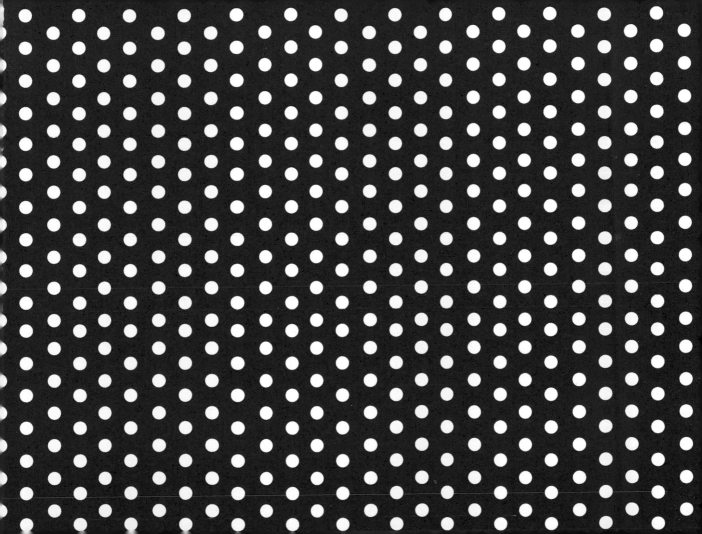

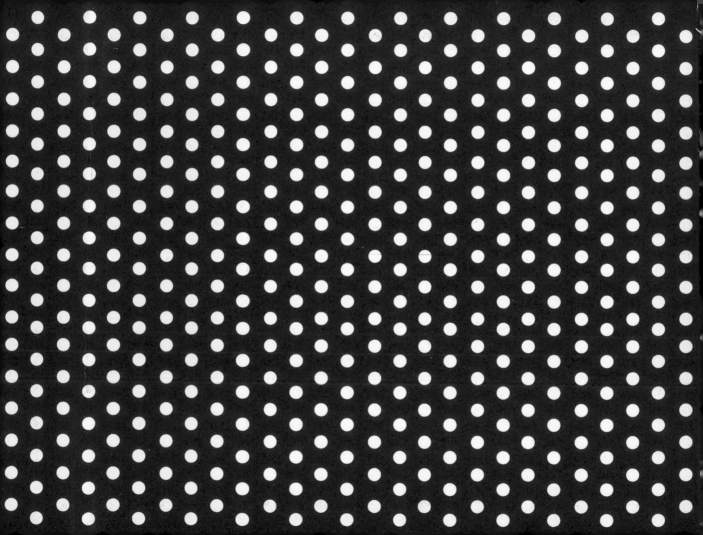